House Cleaning

This Planner Belongs To

Name ....

Contact Info. ....
....
....

This Planner Includes:
- Cleaning Cheat Sheet.
- Daily Cleaning Checklist.
- Weekly Cleaning Planner.
- Monthly Cleaning Checklist.
- Seasonal Cleaning Checklist.
- Special Care Cleaning Instructions log.
- Homemade Cleaners Formulas log.
- Laundry Schedule.

I had to clean my house for two hours just to tell guests, "Sorry about the mess." 😄

Have A Great Day

Weekly Cleaning Cheat Sheet

Bedrooms/Living Areas

- Wash clothes, bed sheets and towels.
- Mop, vacuum or sweep all floors.
- Dust all surfaces.
- Tidy up the living room, fold blankets, stack books and magazines.
- Dust the entertainment center.
- Straighten pillows, blankets, couch cushions etc.
- Organize clutter, sort mail and paperwork.
- Do a load of laundry daily to prevent piles from building up.
- Empty all the wastebaskets throughout the house.
- Collect items that don't belong and return them to the proper place.
- Straighten shelves and cabinets.
- Wipe down and organize toys.
- Water and dust plants.
- Wash pillow covers, couch covers, and blankets.
- Clean under couches, chairs, and other furniture.

Bathrooms

- Scrubbing sinks, tubs, showers, and toilets.
- Sweeping and mopping the floor.
- Clean Mirrors.
- Wash bath mats.
- Clean out drawers and cabinets.
- Thoroughly clean bathrooms.
- Restock toilet paper & soap if needed.
- Wash hand towels.

Kitchen

- Removing items from counter-tops and cleaning the counter-tops with soap and water.
- Wiping down the outside of the items/appliances if they're dirty.
- Cleaning the stove-top.
- Cleaning out the fridge, throwing away food that's gone bad and washing out containers that can be reused.
- Vacuuming and/or mopping floors.
- Dust surfaces and Wipe kitchen cabinets.
- Laundering and replacing dish and hand towels.
- Make a grocery list, visit the store, then put the groceries away.

- Clean stove, oven, and range hood.
- Clean microwave inside and out.
- Organize the fridge, pantry, cupboards and plan meals for the week.
- Clean cycle the dishwasher.

Other

- Mowing the lawn.
- Weeding the garden.
- Taking out the trash.
- Clean cars inside and out.
- Dust light fixtures/ceiling fan/corner cobwebs.
- Clean door handles and dust door-frames.
- Dust windowsills, blinds, picture frames, lampshades, and all furnitures.
- Dust knick-knacks, books, etc.
- Shake out throw rugs.
- Sweep, vacuum or mop floors.
- Wipe off washer and dryer.
- Water and dust plants.
- Organize & Sweep out the garage.
- Wipe down light switches, baseboards and remotes.
- Sweep & organize porch.

Tips

- Stick to a realistic schedule that truly works for you and your home.
- Walk through your home, room by room, taking an inventory of the areas and tasks that will make up your house cleaning schedule.
- Either divide your schedule by room or by doing the same task (like mopping all rooms) for spaces of the house. Clean in one long block or split the schedule over shorter time blocks.
- Clean from top to bottom (ceiling to floors).
- Select cleaning frequency, most spaces probably need a weekly or biweekly cleaning.
- Your cleaning schedule will always be a work in progress, and will get better with time.
- Reevaluate Your Schedule and turn your cleaning tasks into daily habits.
- Make this book your own, and add your personal touch using colors, sticky notes, pencils, stickers.
- Get your family involved, assign jobs to family member helping cleaning the house.
- Arrange your daily tasks into chunks and divide them over the different times of the day.

Daily Cleaning Checklist

Time   Week of: _____

	Mon.	Tue.	Wed.	Thu.	Fri.	Sat.	Sun.

Bedrooms/Living Areas
- Make beds & Remove clutter – Straighten nightstand
- Put away clothing
- Vacuum or sweep as needed
- Straighten all pillows and blankets on the sofa
- Wipe spots and fingerprints from tabletops

Bathrooms
- Clean Mirror, the sink, faucet and other counter-top
- Squeegee or wipe shower door/curtain and walls
- Clean the toilet bowl & Wipe toilet seat / rim
- Replace any stained towels or washcloths

Kitchen
- Taking the trash out
- Wash dishes (load/Unload dishwasher)
- Wipe up spots on the floor & Sweep/mop as needed
- Clean sink, counter-tops, and appliances
- Clean inside microwave/crumb tray of toaster

Other
- Clean litter boxes/pet areas
- Mop/Sweep or vacuum the floors as needed

Weekly Cleaning Planner

Time	Monday		Time	Tuesday

Time	Wednesday		Time	Thursday

Time	Friday		Time	Saturday

Time	Sunday		Remarks / Goals	

Daily Cleaning Checklist

Time   Week of: _____

	Mon.	Tue.	Wed.	Thu.	Fri.	Sat.	Sun.

Bedrooms/Living Areas
- Make beds & Remove clutter - Straighten nightstand
- Put away clothing
- Vacuum or sweep as needed
- Straighten all pillows and blankets on the sofa
- Wipe spots and fingerprints from tabletops

Bathrooms
- Clean Mirror, the sink, faucet and other counter-top
- Squeegee or wipe shower door/curtain and walls
- Clean the toilet bowl & Wipe toilet seat / rim
- Replace any stained towels or washcloths

Kitchen
- Taking the trash out
- Wash dishes (load/Unload dishwasher)
- Wipe up spots on the floor & Sweep/mop as needed
- Clean sink, counter-tops, and appliances
- Clean inside microwave/crumb tray of toaster

Other
- Clean litter boxes/pet areas
- Mop/Sweep or vacuum the floors as needed

Weekly Cleaning Planner

Time	Monday		Time	Tuesday

Time	Wednesday		Time	Thursday

Time	Friday		Time	Saturday

Time	Sunday		Remarks / Goals	

Daily Cleaning Checklist

Time   Week of:_____

	Mon.	Tue.	Wed.	Thu.	Fri.	Sat.	Sun.

Bedrooms/Living Areas

- Make beds & Remove clutter - Straighten nightstand
- Put away clothing
- Vacuum or sweep as needed
- Straighten all pillows and blankets on the sofa
- Wipe spots and fingerprints from tabletops

Bathrooms

- Clean Mirror, the sink, faucet and other counter-top
- Squeegee or wipe shower door/curtain and walls
- Clean the toilet bowl & Wipe toilet seat / rim
- Replace any stained towels or washcloths

Kitchen

- Taking the trash out
- Wash dishes (load/Unload dishwasher)
- Wipe up spots on the floor & Sweep/mop as needed
- Clean sink, counter-tops, and appliances
- Clean inside microwave/crumb tray of toaster

Other

- Clean litter boxes/pet areas
- Mop/Sweep or vacuum the floors as needed

Weekly Cleaning Planner

Time	Monday		Time	Tuesday

Time	Wednesday		Time	Thursday

Time	Friday		Time	Saturday

Time	Sunday		Remarks / Goals	

Daily Cleaning Checklist

Time Week of: _____ Mon. Tue. Wed. Thu. Fri. Sat. Sun.

Bedrooms/Living Areas

- Make beds & Remove clutter - Straighten nightstand
- Put away clothing
- Vacuum or sweep as needed
- Straighten all pillows and blankets on the sofa
- Wipe spots and fingerprints from tabletops

Bathrooms

- Clean Mirror, the sink, faucet and other counter-top
- Squeegee or wipe shower door/curtain and walls
- Clean the toilet bowl & Wipe toilet seat / rim
- Replace any stained towels or washcloths

Kitchen

- Taking the trash out
- Wash dishes (load/Unload dishwasher)
- Wipe up spots on the floor & Sweep/mop as needed
- Clean sink, counter-tops, and appliances
- Clean inside microwave/crumb tray of toaster

Other

- Clean litter boxes/pet areas
- Mop/Sweep or vacuum the floors as needed

Weekly Cleaning Planner

Time	Monday		Time	Tuesday

Time	Wednesday		Time	Thursday

Time	Friday		Time	Saturday

Time	Sunday			Remarks / Goals

Daily Cleaning Checklist

Time Week of: _____

	Mon.	Tue.	Wed.	Thu.	Fri.	Sat.	Sun.

Bedrooms/Living Areas

- Make beds & Remove clutter - Straighten nightstand
- Put away clothing
- Vacuum or sweep as needed
- Straighten all pillows and blankets on the sofa
- Wipe spots and fingerprints from tabletops

Bathrooms

- Clean Mirror, the sink, faucet and other counter-top
- Squeegee or wipe shower door/curtain and walls
- Clean the toilet bowl & Wipe toilet seat / rim
- Replace any stained towels or washcloths

Kitchen

- Taking the trash out
- Wash dishes (load/Unload dishwasher)
- Wipe up spots on the floor & Sweep/mop as needed
- Clean sink, counter-tops, and appliances
- Clean inside microwave/crumb tray of toaster

Other

- Clean litter boxes/pet areas
- Mop/Sweep or vacuum the floors as needed

Weekly Cleaning Planner

Time	Monday		Time	Tuesday

Time	Wednesday		Time	Thursday

Time	Friday		Time	Saturday

Time	Sunday		Remarks / Goals	

Daily Cleaning Checklist

Time   Week of: _____

	Mon.	Tue.	Wed.	Thu.	Fri.	Sat.	Sun.

Bedrooms/Living Areas

- Make beds & Remove clutter - Straighten nightstand
- Put away clothing
- Vacuum or sweep as needed
- Straighten all pillows and blankets on the sofa
- Wipe spots and fingerprints from tabletops

Bathrooms

- Clean Mirror, the sink, faucet and other counter-top
- Squeegee or wipe shower door/curtain and walls
- Clean the toilet bowl & Wipe toilet seat / rim
- Replace any stained towels or washcloths

Kitchen

- Taking the trash out
- Wash dishes (load/Unload dishwasher)
- Wipe up spots on the floor & Sweep/mop as needed
- Clean sink, counter-tops, and appliances
- Clean inside microwave/crumb tray of toaster

Other

- Clean litter boxes/pet areas
- Mop/Sweep or vacuum the floors as needed

Weekly Cleaning Planner

Time	Monday	Time	Tuesday

Time	Wednesday	Time	Thursday

Time	Friday	Time	Saturday

Time	Sunday	Remarks / Goals	

Daily Cleaning Checklist

Time   Week of: _____

Mon. Tue. Wed. Thu. Fri. Sat. Sun.

Bedrooms/Living Areas
- Make beds & Remove clutter - Straighten nightstand
- Put away clothing
- Vacuum or sweep as needed
- Straighten all pillows and blankets on the sofa
- Wipe spots and fingerprints from tabletops

Bathrooms
- Clean Mirror, the sink, faucet and other counter-top
- Squeegee or wipe shower door/curtain and walls
- Clean the toilet bowl & Wipe toilet seat / rim
- Replace any stained towels or washcloths

Kitchen
- Taking the trash out
- Wash dishes (load/Unload dishwasher)
- Wipe up spots on the floor & Sweep/mop as needed
- Clean sink, counter-tops, and appliances
- Clean inside microwave/crumb tray of toaster

Other
- Clean litter boxes/pet areas
- Mop/Sweep or vacuum the floors as needed

Weekly Cleaning Planner

Time	Monday		Time	Tuesday

Time	Wednesday		Time	Thursday

Time	Friday		Time	Saturday

Time	Sunday		Remarks / Goals	

Daily Cleaning Checklist

Time   Week of: _____

	Mon.	Tue.	Wed.	Thu.	Fri.	Sat.	Sun.

Bedrooms/Living Areas

- Make beds & Remove clutter - Straighten nightstand
- Put away clothing
- Vacuum or sweep as needed
- Straighten all pillows and blankets on the sofa
- Wipe spots and fingerprints from tabletops

Bathrooms

- Clean Mirror, the sink, faucet and other counter-top
- Squeegee or wipe shower door/curtain and walls
- Clean the toilet bowl & Wipe toilet seat / rim
- Replace any stained towels or washcloths

Kitchen

- Taking the trash out
- Wash dishes (load/Unload dishwasher)
- Wipe up spots on the floor & Sweep/mop as needed
- Clean sink, counter-tops, and appliances
- Clean inside microwave/crumb tray of toaster

Other

- Clean litter boxes/pet areas
- Mop/Sweep or vacuum the floors as needed

Weekly Cleaning Planner

Time	Monday		Time	Tuesday

Time	Wednesday		Time	Thursday

Time	Friday		Time	Saturday

Time	Sunday		Remarks / Goals	

Daily Cleaning Checklist

Time   Week of: _____

	Task	Mon.	Tue.	Wed.	Thu.	Fri.	Sat.	Sun.
Bedrooms/Living Areas	Make beds & Remove clutter - Straighten nightstand	☐	☐	☐	☐	☐	☐	☐
	Put away clothing	☐	☐	☐	☐	☐	☐	☐
	Vacuum or sweep as needed	☐	☐	☐	☐	☐	☐	☐
	Straighten all pillows and blankets on the sofa	☐	☐	☐	☐	☐	☐	☐
	Wipe spots and fingerprints from tabletops	☐	☐	☐	☐	☐	☐	☐
Bathrooms	Clean Mirror, the sink, faucet and other counter-top	☐	☐	☐	☐	☐	☐	☐
	Squeegee or wipe shower door/curtain and walls	☐	☐	☐	☐	☐	☐	☐
	Clean the toilet bowl & Wipe toilet seat / rim	☐	☐	☐	☐	☐	☐	☐
	Replace any stained towels or washcloths	☐	☐	☐	☐	☐	☐	☐
Kitchen	Taking the trash out	☐	☐	☐	☐	☐	☐	☐
	Wash dishes (load/Unload dishwasher)	☐	☐	☐	☐	☐	☐	☐
	Wipe up spots on the floor & Sweep/mop as needed	☐	☐	☐	☐	☐	☐	☐
	Clean sink, counter-tops, and appliances	☐	☐	☐	☐	☐	☐	☐
	Clean inside microwave/crumb tray of toaster	☐	☐	☐	☐	☐	☐	☐
Other	Clean litter boxes/pet areas	☐	☐	☐	☐	☐	☐	☐
	Mop/Sweep or vacuum the floors as needed	☐	☐	☐	☐	☐	☐	☐

Weekly Cleaning Planner

Time	Monday		Time	Tuesday

Time	Wednesday		Time	Thursday

Time	Friday		Time	Saturday

Time	Sunday		Remarks / Goals	

Daily Cleaning Checklist

Time   Week of: _____

	Mon.	Tue.	Wed.	Thu.	Fri.	Sat.	Sun.

Bedrooms/Living Areas
- Make beds & Remove clutter - Straighten nightstand
- Put away clothing
- Vacuum or sweep as needed
- Straighten all pillows and blankets on the sofa
- Wipe spots and fingerprints from tabletops

Bathrooms
- Clean Mirror, the sink, faucet and other counter-top
- Squeegee or wipe shower door/curtain and walls
- Clean the toilet bowl & Wipe toilet seat / rim
- Replace any stained towels or washcloths

Kitchen
- Taking the trash out
- Wash dishes (load/Unload dishwasher)
- Wipe up spots on the floor & Sweep/mop as needed
- Clean sink, counter-tops, and appliances
- Clean inside microwave/crumb tray of toaster

Other
- Clean litter boxes/pet areas
- Mop/Sweep or vacuum the floors as needed

Weekly Cleaning Planner

Time	Monday		Time	Tuesday

Time	Wednesday		Time	Thursday

Time	Friday		Time	Saturday

Time	Sunday			Remarks / Goals

Daily Cleaning Checklist

Time   Week of: _____   Mon. Tue. Wed. Thu. Fri. Sat. Sun.

Bedrooms/Living Areas
- Make beds & Remove clutter - Straighten nightstand
- Put away clothing
- Vacuum or sweep as needed
- Straighten all pillows and blankets on the sofa
- Wipe spots and fingerprints from tabletops

Bathrooms
- Clean Mirror, the sink, faucet and other counter-top
- Squeegee or wipe shower door/curtain and walls
- Clean the toilet bowl & Wipe toilet seat / rim
- Replace any stained towels or washcloths

Kitchen
- Taking the trash out
- Wash dishes (load/Unload dishwasher)
- Wipe up spots on the floor & Sweep/mop as needed
- Clean sink, counter-tops, and appliances
- Clean inside microwave/crumb tray of toaster

Other
- Clean litter boxes/pet areas
- Mop/Sweep or vacuum the floors as needed

Weekly Cleaning Planner

Time	Monday		Time	Tuesday

Time	Wednesday		Time	Thursday

Time	Friday		Time	Saturday

Time	Sunday		Remarks / Goals	

Daily Cleaning Checklist

Time   Week of: _____

	Mon.	Tue.	Wed.	Thu.	Fri.	Sat.	Sun.

Bedrooms/Living Areas
- Make beds & Remove clutter - Straighten nightstand
- Put away clothing
- Vacuum or sweep as needed
- Straighten all pillows and blankets on the sofa
- Wipe spots and fingerprints from tabletops

Bathrooms
- Clean Mirror, the sink, faucet and other counter-top
- Squeegee or wipe shower door/curtain and walls
- Clean the toilet bowl & Wipe toilet seat / rim
- Replace any stained towels or washcloths

Kitchen
- Taking the trash out
- Wash dishes (load/Unload dishwasher)
- Wipe up spots on the floor & Sweep/mop as needed
- Clean sink, counter-tops, and appliances
- Clean inside microwave/crumb tray of toaster

Other
- Clean litter boxes/pet areas
- Mop/Sweep or vacuum the floors as needed

Weekly Cleaning Planner

Time	Monday

Time	Tuesday

Time	Wednesday

Time	Thursday

Time	Friday

Time	Saturday

Time	Sunday

Remarks / Goals

Daily Cleaning Checklist

Time   Week of: _____

	Mon.	Tue.	Wed.	Thu.	Fri.	Sat.	Sun.

Bedrooms/Living Areas
- Make beds & Remove clutter - Straighten nightstand
- Put away clothing
- Vacuum or sweep as needed
- Straighten all pillows and blankets on the sofa
- Wipe spots and fingerprints from tabletops

Bathrooms
- Clean Mirror, the sink, faucet and other counter-top
- Squeegee or wipe shower door/curtain and walls
- Clean the toilet bowl & Wipe toilet seat / rim
- Replace any stained towels or washcloths

Kitchen
- Taking the trash out
- Wash dishes (load/Unload dishwasher)
- Wipe up spots on the floor & Sweep/mop as needed
- Clean sink, counter-tops, and appliances
- Clean inside microwave/crumb tray of toaster

Other
- Clean litter boxes/pet areas
- Mop/Sweep or vacuum the floors as needed

Weekly Cleaning Planner

Time	Monday		Time	Tuesday

Time	Wednesday		Time	Thursday

Time	Friday		Time	Saturday

Time	Sunday			Remarks / Goals

Daily Cleaning Checklist

Time   Week of:_____

	Mon.	Tue.	Wed.	Thu.	Fri.	Sat.	Sun.

Bedrooms/Living Areas

- Make beds & Remove clutter – Straighten nightstand
- Put away clothing
- Vacuum or sweep as needed
- Straighten all pillows and blankets on the sofa
- Wipe spots and fingerprints from tabletops

Bathrooms

- Clean Mirror, the sink, faucet and other counter-top
- Squeegee or wipe shower door/curtain and walls
- Clean the toilet bowl & Wipe toilet seat / rim
- Replace any stained towels or washcloths

Kitchen

- Taking the trash out
- Wash dishes (load/Unload dishwasher)
- Wipe up spots on the floor & Sweep/mop as needed
- Clean sink, counter-tops, and appliances
- Clean inside microwave/crumb tray of toaster

Other

- Clean litter boxes/pet areas
- Mop/Sweep or vacuum the floors as needed

Weekly Cleaning Planner

Time	Monday

Time	Tuesday

Time	Wednesday

Time	Thursday

Time	Friday

Time	Saturday

Time	Sunday

Remarks / Goals

Daily Cleaning Checklist

Time   Week of: _____

	Mon.	Tue.	Wed.	Thu.	Fri.	Sat.	Sun.

Bedrooms/Living Areas
- Make beds & Remove clutter - Straighten nightstand
- Put away clothing
- Vacuum or sweep as needed
- Straighten all pillows and blankets on the sofa
- Wipe spots and fingerprints from tabletops

Bathrooms
- Clean Mirror, the sink, faucet and other counter-top
- Squeegee or wipe shower door/curtain and walls
- Clean the toilet bowl & Wipe toilet seat / rim
- Replace any stained towels or washcloths

Kitchen
- Taking the trash out
- Wash dishes (load/Unload dishwasher)
- Wipe up spots on the floor & Sweep/mop as needed
- Clean sink, counter-tops, and appliances
- Clean inside microwave/crumb tray of toaster

Other
- Clean litter boxes/pet areas
- Mop/Sweep or vacuum the floors as needed

Weekly Cleaning Planner

Time	Monday		Time	Tuesday

Time	Wednesday		Time	Thursday

Time	Friday		Time	Saturday

Time	Sunday			Remarks / Goals

Daily Cleaning Checklist

Time   Week of: _____

	Task	Mon.	Tue.	Wed.	Thu.	Fri.	Sat.	Sun.
Bedrooms/Living Areas	Make beds & Remove clutter - Straighten nightstand	☐	☐	☐	☐	☐	☐	☐
	Put away clothing	☐	☐	☐	☐	☐	☐	☐
		☐	☐	☐	☐	☐	☐	☐
		☐	☐	☐	☐	☐	☐	☐
	Vacuum or sweep as needed	☐	☐	☐	☐	☐	☐	☐
	Straighten all pillows and blankets on the sofa	☐	☐	☐	☐	☐	☐	☐
	Wipe spots and fingerprints from tabletops	☐	☐	☐	☐	☐	☐	☐
		☐	☐	☐	☐	☐	☐	☐
		☐	☐	☐	☐	☐	☐	☐
		☐	☐	☐	☐	☐	☐	☐
		☐	☐	☐	☐	☐	☐	☐
Bathrooms	Clean Mirror, the sink, faucet and other counter-top	☐	☐	☐	☐	☐	☐	☐
	Squeegee or wipe shower door/curtain and walls	☐	☐	☐	☐	☐	☐	☐
	Clean the toilet bowl & Wipe toilet seat / rim	☐	☐	☐	☐	☐	☐	☐
	Replace any stained towels or washcloths	☐	☐	☐	☐	☐	☐	☐
		☐	☐	☐	☐	☐	☐	☐
		☐	☐	☐	☐	☐	☐	☐
		☐	☐	☐	☐	☐	☐	☐
Kitchen	Taking the trash out	☐	☐	☐	☐	☐	☐	☐
	Wash dishes (load/Unload dishwasher)	☐	☐	☐	☐	☐	☐	☐
	Wipe up spots on the floor & Sweep/mop as needed	☐	☐	☐	☐	☐	☐	☐
	Clean sink, counter-tops, and appliances	☐	☐	☐	☐	☐	☐	☐
	Clean inside microwave/crumb tray of toaster	☐	☐	☐	☐	☐	☐	☐
		☐	☐	☐	☐	☐	☐	☐
		☐	☐	☐	☐	☐	☐	☐
Other	Clean litter boxes/pet areas	☐	☐	☐	☐	☐	☐	☐
	Mop/Sweep or vacuum the floors as needed	☐	☐	☐	☐	☐	☐	☐
		☐	☐	☐	☐	☐	☐	☐
		☐	☐	☐	☐	☐	☐	☐
		☐	☐	☐	☐	☐	☐	☐

Weekly Cleaning Planner

Time	Monday		Time	Tuesday

Time	Wednesday		Time	Thursday

Time	Friday		Time	Saturday

Time	Sunday			Remarks / Goals

Daily Cleaning Checklist

Time   Week of:_____

	Mon.	Tue.	Wed.	Thu.	Fri.	Sat.	Sun.

Bedrooms/Living Areas
- Make beds & Remove clutter - Straighten nightstand
- Put away clothing
- Vacuum or sweep as needed
- Straighten all pillows and blankets on the sofa
- Wipe spots and fingerprints from tabletops

Bathrooms
- Clean Mirror, the sink, faucet and other counter-top
- Squeegee or wipe shower door/curtain and walls
- Clean the toilet bowl & Wipe toilet seat / rim
- Replace any stained towels or washcloths

Kitchen
- Taking the trash out
- Wash dishes (load/Unload dishwasher)
- Wipe up spots on the floor & Sweep/mop as needed
- Clean sink, counter-tops, and appliances
- Clean inside microwave/crumb tray of toaster

Other
- Clean litter boxes/pet areas
- Mop/Sweep or vacuum the floors as needed

Weekly Cleaning Planner

Time	Monday		Time	Tuesday

Time	Wednesday		Time	Thursday

Time	Friday		Time	Saturday

Time	Sunday		Remarks / Goals	

Daily Cleaning Checklist

Time   Week of:_____

	Mon.	Tue.	Wed.	Thu.	Fri.	Sat.	Sun.

Bedrooms/Living Areas
- Make beds & Remove clutter - Straighten nightstand
- Put away clothing
- Vacuum or sweep as needed
- Straighten all pillows and blankets on the sofa
- Wipe spots and fingerprints from tabletops

Bathrooms
- Clean Mirror, the sink, faucet and other counter-top
- Squeegee or wipe shower door/curtain and walls
- Clean the toilet bowl & Wipe toilet seat / rim
- Replace any stained towels or washcloths

Kitchen
- Taking the trash out
- Wash dishes (load/Unload dishwasher)
- Wipe up spots on the floor & Sweep/mop as needed
- Clean sink, counter-tops, and appliances
- Clean inside microwave/crumb tray of toaster

Other
- Clean litter boxes/pet areas
- Mop/Sweep or vacuum the floors as needed

Weekly Cleaning Planner

Time	Monday

Time	Tuesday

Time	Wednesday

Time	Thursday

Time	Friday

Time	Saturday

Time	Sunday

Remarks / Goals

Daily Cleaning Checklist

Time　　　　　　　　　　　　　　Week of:_____

	Mon.	Tue.	Wed.	Thu.	Fri.	Sat.	Sun.

Bedrooms/Living Areas

- Make beds & Remove clutter – Straighten nightstand
- Put away clothing
- Vacuum or sweep as needed
- Straighten all pillows and blankets on the sofa
- Wipe spots and fingerprints from tabletops

Bathrooms

- Clean Mirror, the sink, faucet and other counter-top
- Squeegee or wipe shower door/curtain and walls
- Clean the toilet bowl & Wipe toilet seat / rim
- Replace any stained towels or washcloths

Kitchen

- Taking the trash out
- Wash dishes (load/Unload dishwasher)
- Wipe up spots on the floor & Sweep/mop as needed
- Clean sink, counter-tops, and appliances
- Clean inside microwave/crumb tray of toaster

Other

- Clean litter boxes/pet areas
- Mop/Sweep or vacuum the floors as needed

Weekly Cleaning Planner

Time	Monday		Time	Tuesday

Time	Wednesday		Time	Thursday

Time	Friday		Time	Saturday

Time	Sunday		Remarks / Goals	

Daily Cleaning Checklist

Time Week of:_____

	Mon.	Tue.	Wed.	Thu.	Fri.	Sat.	Sun.

Bedrooms/Living Areas
- Make beds & Remove clutter - Straighten nightstand
- Put away clothing
- Vacuum or sweep as needed
- Straighten all pillows and blankets on the sofa
- Wipe spots and fingerprints from tabletops

Bathrooms
- Clean Mirror, the sink, faucet and other counter-top
- Squeegee or wipe shower door/curtain and walls
- Clean the toilet bowl & Wipe toilet seat / rim
- Replace any stained towels or washcloths

Kitchen
- Taking the trash out
- Wash dishes (load/Unload dishwasher)
- Wipe up spots on the floor & Sweep/mop as needed
- Clean sink, counter-tops, and appliances
- Clean inside microwave/crumb tray of toaster

Other
- Clean litter boxes/pet areas
- Mop/Sweep or vacuum the floors as needed

Weekly Cleaning Planner

Time	Monday

Time	Tuesday

Time	Wednesday

Time	Thursday

Time	Friday

Time	Saturday

Time	Sunday

Remarks / Goals

Daily Cleaning Checklist

Time   Week of:_____

	Mon.	Tue.	Wed.	Thu.	Fri.	Sat.	Sun.

Bedrooms/Living Areas

- Make beds & Remove clutter - Straighten nightstand
- Put away clothing
- Vacuum or sweep as needed
- Straighten all pillows and blankets on the sofa
- Wipe spots and fingerprints from tabletops

Bathrooms

- Clean Mirror, the sink, faucet and other counter-top
- Squeegee or wipe shower door/curtain and walls
- Clean the toilet bowl & Wipe toilet seat / rim
- Replace any stained towels or washcloths

Kitchen

- Taking the trash out
- Wash dishes (load/Unload dishwasher)
- Wipe up spots on the floor & Sweep/mop as needed
- Clean sink, counter-tops, and appliances
- Clean inside microwave/crumb tray of toaster

Other

- Clean litter boxes/pet areas
- Mop/Sweep or vacuum the floors as needed

Weekly Cleaning Planner

Time	Monday		Time	Tuesday

Time	Wednesday		Time	Thursday

Time	Friday		Time	Saturday

Time	Sunday		Remarks / Goals	

Daily Cleaning Checklist

Time   Week of: _____

	Mon.	Tue.	Wed.	Thu.	Fri.	Sat.	Sun.

Bedrooms/Living Areas

- Make beds & Remove clutter - Straighten nightstand
- Put away clothing
- Vacuum or sweep as needed
- Straighten all pillows and blankets on the sofa
- Wipe spots and fingerprints from tabletops

Bathrooms

- Clean Mirror, the sink, faucet and other counter-top
- Squeegee or wipe shower door/curtain and walls
- Clean the toilet bowl & Wipe toilet seat / rim
- Replace any stained towels or washcloths

Kitchen

- Taking the trash out
- Wash dishes (load/Unload dishwasher)
- Wipe up spots on the floor & Sweep/mop as needed
- Clean sink, counter-tops, and appliances
- Clean inside microwave/crumb tray of toaster

Other

- Clean litter boxes/pet areas
- Mop/Sweep or vacuum the floors as needed

Weekly Cleaning Planner

Time	Monday		Time	Tuesday

Time	Wednesday		Time	Thursday

Time	Friday		Time	Saturday

Time	Sunday		Remarks / Goals	

Daily Cleaning Checklist

Time   Week of: _____

	Mon.	Tue.	Wed.	Thu.	Fri.	Sat.	Sun.

Bedrooms/Living Areas
- Make beds & Remove clutter – Straighten nightstand
- Put away clothing
- Vacuum or sweep as needed
- Straighten all pillows and blankets on the sofa
- Wipe spots and fingerprints from tabletops

Bathrooms
- Clean Mirror, the sink, faucet and other counter-top
- Squeegee or wipe shower door/curtain and walls
- Clean the toilet bowl & Wipe toilet seat / rim
- Replace any stained towels or washcloths

Kitchen
- Taking the trash out
- Wash dishes (load/Unload dishwasher)
- Wipe up spots on the floor & Sweep/mop as needed
- Clean sink, counter-tops, and appliances
- Clean inside microwave/crumb tray of toaster

Other
- Clean litter boxes/pet areas
- Mop/Sweep or vacuum the floors as needed

Weekly Cleaning Planner

Time	Monday		Time	Tuesday

Time	Wednesday		Time	Thursday

Time	Friday		Time	Saturday

Time	Sunday		Remarks / Goals	

Daily Cleaning Checklist

Time　　　　　　　　　　　　Week of:_____

| | Mon. | Tue. | Wed. | Thu. | Fri. | Sat. | Sun. |

Bedrooms/Living Areas
- Make beds & Remove clutter - Straighten nightstand
- Put away clothing
- Vacuum or sweep as needed
- Straighten all pillows and blankets on the sofa
- Wipe spots and fingerprints from tabletops

Bathrooms
- Clean Mirror, the sink, faucet and other counter-top
- Squeegee or wipe shower door/curtain and walls
- Clean the toilet bowl & Wipe toilet seat / rim
- Replace any stained towels or washcloths

Kitchen
- Taking the trash out
- Wash dishes (load/Unload dishwasher)
- Wipe up spots on the floor & Sweep/mop as needed
- Clean sink, counter-tops, and appliances
- Clean inside microwave/crumb tray of toaster

Other
- Clean litter boxes/pet areas
- Mop/Sweep or vacuum the floors as needed

Weekly Cleaning Planner

Time	Monday

Time	Tuesday

Time	Wednesday

Time	Thursday

Time	Friday

Time	Saturday

Time	Sunday

Remarks / Goals

Daily Cleaning Checklist

Time   Week of:_____

	Mon.	Tue.	Wed.	Thu.	Fri.	Sat.	Sun.

Bedrooms/Living Areas

- Make beds & Remove clutter - Straighten nightstand
- Put away clothing
- Vacuum or sweep as needed
- Straighten all pillows and blankets on the sofa
- Wipe spots and fingerprints from tabletops

Bathrooms

- Clean Mirror, the sink, faucet and other counter-top
- Squeegee or wipe shower door/curtain and walls
- Clean the toilet bowl & Wipe toilet seat / rim
- Replace any stained towels or washcloths

Kitchen

- Taking the trash out
- Wash dishes (load/Unload dishwasher)
- Wipe up spots on the floor & Sweep/mop as needed
- Clean sink, counter-tops, and appliances
- Clean inside microwave/crumb tray of toaster

Other

- Clean litter boxes/pet areas
- Mop/Sweep or vacuum the floors as needed

Weekly Cleaning Planner

Time	Monday		Time	Tuesday

Time	Wednesday		Time	Thursday

Time	Friday		Time	Saturday

Time	Sunday			Remarks / Goals

Daily Cleaning Checklist

Time   Week of:_____

| | Mon. | Tue. | Wed. | Thu. | Fri. | Sat. | Sun. |

Bedrooms/Living Areas

- Make beds & Remove clutter – Straighten nightstand
- Put away clothing
- Vacuum or sweep as needed
- Straighten all pillows and blankets on the sofa
- Wipe spots and fingerprints from tabletops

Bathrooms

- Clean Mirror, the sink, faucet and other counter-top
- Squeegee or wipe shower door/curtain and walls
- Clean the toilet bowl & Wipe toilet seat / rim
- Replace any stained towels or washcloths

Kitchen

- Taking the trash out
- Wash dishes (load/Unload dishwasher)
- Wipe up spots on the floor & Sweep/mop as needed
- Clean sink, counter-tops, and appliances
- Clean inside microwave/crumb tray of toaster

Other

- Clean litter boxes/pet areas
- Mop/Sweep or vacuum the floors as needed

Weekly Cleaning Planner

Time	Monday		Time	Tuesday

Time	Wednesday		Time	Thursday

Time	Friday		Time	Saturday

Time	Sunday		Remarks / Goals	

Daily Cleaning Checklist

Time   Week of: _____

	Mon.	Tue.	Wed.	Thu.	Fri.	Sat.	Sun.

Bedrooms/Living Areas
- Make beds & Remove clutter - Straighten nightstand
- Put away clothing
- Vacuum or sweep as needed
- Straighten all pillows and blankets on the sofa
- Wipe spots and fingerprints from tabletops

Bathrooms
- Clean Mirror, the sink, faucet and other counter-top
- Squeegee or wipe shower door/curtain and walls
- Clean the toilet bowl & Wipe toilet seat / rim
- Replace any stained towels or washcloths

Kitchen
- Taking the trash out
- Wash dishes (load/Unload dishwasher)
- Wipe up spots on the floor & Sweep/mop as needed
- Clean sink, counter-tops, and appliances
- Clean inside microwave/crumb tray of toaster

Other
- Clean litter boxes/pet areas
- Mop/Sweep or vacuum the floors as needed

Weekly Cleaning Planner

Time	Monday		Time	Tuesday

Time	Wednesday		Time	Thursday

Time	Friday		Time	Saturday

Time	Sunday			Remarks / Goals

Daily Cleaning Checklist

Time   Week of: _____

Mon. Tue. Wed. Thu. Fri. Sat. Sun.

Bedrooms/Living Areas

- Make beds & Remove clutter - Straighten nightstand
- Put away clothing
- Vacuum or sweep as needed
- Straighten all pillows and blankets on the sofa
- Wipe spots and fingerprints from tabletops

Bathrooms

- Clean Mirror, the sink, faucet and other counter-top
- Squeegee or wipe shower door/curtain and walls
- Clean the toilet bowl & Wipe toilet seat / rim
- Replace any stained towels or washcloths

Kitchen

- Taking the trash out
- Wash dishes (load/Unload dishwasher)
- Wipe up spots on the floor & Sweep/mop as needed
- Clean sink, counter-tops, and appliances
- Clean inside microwave/crumb tray of toaster

Other

- Clean litter boxes/pet areas
- Mop/Sweep or vacuum the floors as needed

Weekly Cleaning Planner

Time	Monday

Time	Tuesday

Time	Wednesday

Time	Thursday

Time	Friday

Time	Saturday

Time	Sunday

Remarks / Goals

Daily Cleaning Checklist

Time Week of: _____

	Mon.	Tue.	Wed.	Thu.	Fri.	Sat.	Sun.

Bedrooms/Living Areas
- Make beds & Remove clutter – Straighten nightstand
- Put away clothing
- Vacuum or sweep as needed
- Straighten all pillows and blankets on the sofa
- Wipe spots and fingerprints from tabletops

Bathrooms
- Clean Mirror, the sink, faucet and other counter-top
- Squeegee or wipe shower door/curtain and walls
- Clean the toilet bowl & Wipe toilet seat / rim
- Replace any stained towels or washcloths

Kitchen
- Taking the trash out
- Wash dishes (load/Unload dishwasher)
- Wipe up spots on the floor & Sweep/mop as needed
- Clean sink, counter-tops, and appliances
- Clean inside microwave/crumb tray of toaster

Other
- Clean litter boxes/pet areas
- Mop/Sweep or vacuum the floors as needed

Weekly Cleaning Planner

Time	Monday		Time	Tuesday

Time	Wednesday		Time	Thursday

Time	Friday		Time	Saturday

Time	Sunday			Remarks / Goals

Daily Cleaning Checklist

Time   Week of: _____

	Mon.	Tue.	Wed.	Thu.	Fri.	Sat.	Sun.

Bedrooms/Living Areas

- Make beds & Remove clutter - Straighten nightstand
- Put away clothing
- Vacuum or sweep as needed
- Straighten all pillows and blankets on the sofa
- Wipe spots and fingerprints from tabletops

Bathrooms

- Clean Mirror, the sink, faucet and other counter-top
- Squeegee or wipe shower door/curtain and walls
- Clean the toilet bowl & Wipe toilet seat / rim
- Replace any stained towels or washcloths

Kitchen

- Taking the trash out
- Wash dishes (load/Unload dishwasher)
- Wipe up spots on the floor & Sweep/mop as needed
- Clean sink, counter-tops, and appliances
- Clean inside microwave/crumb tray of toaster

Other

- Clean litter boxes/pet areas
- Mop/Sweep or vacuum the floors as needed

Weekly Cleaning Planner

Time	Monday		Time	Tuesday

Time	Wednesday		Time	Thursday

Time	Friday		Time	Saturday

Time	Sunday			Remarks / Goals

Daily Cleaning Checklist

Time   Week of: _____

	Mon.	Tue.	Wed.	Thu.	Fri.	Sat.	Sun.

Bedrooms/Living Areas
- Make beds & Remove clutter - Straighten nightstand
- Put away clothing
- Vacuum or sweep as needed
- Straighten all pillows and blankets on the sofa
- Wipe spots and fingerprints from tabletops

Bathrooms
- Clean Mirror, the sink, faucet and other counter-top
- Squeegee or wipe shower door/curtain and walls
- Clean the toilet bowl & Wipe toilet seat / rim
- Replace any stained towels or washcloths

Kitchen
- Taking the trash out
- Wash dishes (load/Unload dishwasher)
- Wipe up spots on the floor & Sweep/mop as needed
- Clean sink, counter-tops, and appliances
- Clean inside microwave/crumb tray of toaster

Other
- Clean litter boxes/pet areas
- Mop/Sweep or vacuum the floors as needed

Weekly Cleaning Planner

Time	Monday

Time	Tuesday

Time	Wednesday

Time	Thursday

Time	Friday

Time	Saturday

Time	Sunday

Remarks / Goals

Daily Cleaning Checklist

Time   Week of:_____

	Mon.	Tue.	Wed.	Thu.	Fri.	Sat.	Sun.

Bedrooms/Living Areas
- Make beds & Remove clutter - Straighten nightstand
- Put away clothing
- Vacuum or sweep as needed
- Straighten all pillows and blankets on the sofa
- Wipe spots and fingerprints from tabletops

Bathrooms
- Clean Mirror, the sink, faucet and other counter-top
- Squeegee or wipe shower door/curtain and walls
- Clean the toilet bowl & Wipe toilet seat / rim
- Replace any stained towels or washcloths

Kitchen
- Taking the trash out
- Wash dishes (load/Unload dishwasher)
- Wipe up spots on the floor & Sweep/mop as needed
- Clean sink, counter-tops, and appliances
- Clean inside microwave/crumb tray of toaster

Other
- Clean litter boxes/pet areas
- Mop/Sweep or vacuum the floors as needed

Weekly Cleaning Planner

Time	Monday		Time	Tuesday

Time	Wednesday		Time	Thursday

Time	Friday		Time	Saturday

Time	Sunday		Remarks / Goals	

Daily Cleaning Checklist

Time   Week of: _____

	Mon.	Tue.	Wed.	Thu.	Fri.	Sat.	Sun.

Bedrooms/Living Areas
- Make beds & Remove clutter - Straighten nightstand
- Put away clothing
- Vacuum or sweep as needed
- Straighten all pillows and blankets on the sofa
- Wipe spots and fingerprints from tabletops

Bathrooms
- Clean Mirror, the sink, faucet and other counter-top
- Squeegee or wipe shower door/curtain and walls
- Clean the toilet bowl & Wipe toilet seat / rim
- Replace any stained towels or washcloths

Kitchen
- Taking the trash out
- Wash dishes (load/Unload dishwasher)
- Wipe up spots on the floor & Sweep/mop as needed
- Clean sink, counter-tops, and appliances
- Clean inside microwave/crumb tray of toaster

Other
- Clean litter boxes/pet areas
- Mop/Sweep or vacuum the floors as needed

Weekly Cleaning Planner

Time	Monday		Time	Tuesday

Time	Wednesday		Time	Thursday

Time	Friday		Time	Saturday

Time	Sunday		Remarks / Goals	

Daily Cleaning Checklist

Time   Week of:_____

	Mon.	Tue.	Wed.	Thu.	Fri.	Sat.	Sun.

Bedrooms/Living Areas

- Make beds & Remove clutter - Straighten nightstand
- Put away clothing
- Vacuum or sweep as needed
- Straighten all pillows and blankets on the sofa
- Wipe spots and fingerprints from tabletops

Bathrooms

- Clean Mirror, the sink, faucet and other counter-top
- Squeegee or wipe shower door/curtain and walls
- Clean the toilet bowl & Wipe toilet seat / rim
- Replace any stained towels or washcloths

Kitchen

- Taking the trash out
- Wash dishes (load/Unload dishwasher)
- Wipe up spots on the floor & Sweep/mop as needed
- Clean sink, counter-tops, and appliances
- Clean inside microwave/crumb tray of toaster

Other

- Clean litter boxes/pet areas
- Mop/Sweep or vacuum the floors as needed

Weekly Cleaning Planner

Time	Monday		Time	Tuesday

Time	Wednesday		Time	Thursday

Time	Friday		Time	Saturday

Time	Sunday		Remarks / Goals	

Daily Cleaning Checklist

Time   Week of: _____

	Mon.	Tue.	Wed.	Thu.	Fri.	Sat.	Sun.

Bedrooms/Living Areas

- Make beds & Remove clutter - Straighten nightstand
- Put away clothing
- Vacuum or sweep as needed
- Straighten all pillows and blankets on the sofa
- Wipe spots and fingerprints from tabletops

Bathrooms

- Clean Mirror, the sink, faucet and other counter-top
- Squeegee or wipe shower door/curtain and walls
- Clean the toilet bowl & Wipe toilet seat / rim
- Replace any stained towels or washcloths

Kitchen

- Taking the trash out
- Wash dishes (load/Unload dishwasher)
- Wipe up spots on the floor & Sweep/mop as needed
- Clean sink, counter-tops, and appliances
- Clean inside microwave/crumb tray of toaster

Other

- Clean litter boxes/pet areas
- Mop/Sweep or vacuum the floors as needed

Weekly Cleaning Planner

Time	Monday		Time	Tuesday

Time	Wednesday		Time	Thursday

Time	Friday		Time	Saturday

Time	Sunday		Remarks / Goals	

Daily Cleaning Checklist

Time   Week of: _____

Mon. Tue. Wed. Thu. Fri. Sat. Sun.

Bedrooms/Living Areas

- Make beds & Remove clutter - Straighten nightstand
- Put away clothing
- Vacuum or sweep as needed
- Straighten all pillows and blankets on the sofa
- Wipe spots and fingerprints from tabletops

Bathrooms

- Clean Mirror, the sink, faucet and other counter-top
- Squeegee or wipe shower door/curtain and walls
- Clean the toilet bowl & Wipe toilet seat / rim
- Replace any stained towels or washcloths

Kitchen

- Taking the trash out
- Wash dishes (load/Unload dishwasher)
- Wipe up spots on the floor & Sweep/mop as needed
- Clean sink, counter-tops, and appliances
- Clean inside microwave/crumb tray of toaster

Other

- Clean litter boxes/pet areas
- Mop/Sweep or vacuum the floors as needed

Weekly Cleaning Planner

Time	Monday

Time	Tuesday

Time	Wednesday

Time	Thursday

Time	Friday

Time	Saturday

Time	Sunday

Remarks / Goals

Daily Cleaning Checklist

Time   Week of: _____

		Mon.	Tue.	Wed.	Thu.	Fri.	Sat.	Sun.
Bedrooms/Living Areas	Make beds & Remove clutter - Straighten nightstand	☐	☐	☐	☐	☐	☐	☐
	Put away clothing	☐	☐	☐	☐	☐	☐	☐
	Vacuum or sweep as needed	☐	☐	☐	☐	☐	☐	☐
	Straighten all pillows and blankets on the sofa	☐	☐	☐	☐	☐	☐	☐
	Wipe spots and fingerprints from tabletops	☐	☐	☐	☐	☐	☐	☐
Bathrooms	Clean Mirror, the sink, faucet and other counter-top	☐	☐	☐	☐	☐	☐	☐
	Squeegee or wipe shower door/curtain and walls	☐	☐	☐	☐	☐	☐	☐
	Clean the toilet bowl & Wipe toilet seat / rim	☐	☐	☐	☐	☐	☐	☐
	Replace any stained towels or washcloths	☐	☐	☐	☐	☐	☐	☐
Kitchen	Taking the trash out	☐	☐	☐	☐	☐	☐	☐
	Wash dishes (load/Unload dishwasher)	☐	☐	☐	☐	☐	☐	☐
	Wipe up spots on the floor & Sweep/mop as needed	☐	☐	☐	☐	☐	☐	☐
	Clean sink, counter-tops, and appliances	☐	☐	☐	☐	☐	☐	☐
	Clean inside microwave/crumb tray of toaster	☐	☐	☐	☐	☐	☐	☐
Other	Clean litter boxes/pet areas	☐	☐	☐	☐	☐	☐	☐
	Mop/Sweep or vacuum the floors as needed	☐	☐	☐	☐	☐	☐	☐

Weekly Cleaning Planner

Time	Monday		Time	Tuesday

Time	Wednesday		Time	Thursday

Time	Friday		Time	Saturday

Time	Sunday			Remarks / Goals

Daily Cleaning Checklist

Time   Week of:_____

	Mon.	Tue.	Wed.	Thu.	Fri.	Sat.	Sun.

Bedrooms/Living Areas

- Make beds & Remove clutter – Straighten nightstand
- Put away clothing
- Vacuum or sweep as needed
- Straighten all pillows and blankets on the sofa
- Wipe spots and fingerprints from tabletops

Bathrooms

- Clean Mirror, the sink, faucet and other counter-top
- Squeegee or wipe shower door/curtain and walls
- Clean the toilet bowl & Wipe toilet seat / rim
- Replace any stained towels or washcloths

Kitchen

- Taking the trash out
- Wash dishes (load/Unload dishwasher)
- Wipe up spots on the floor & Sweep/mop as needed
- Clean sink, counter-tops, and appliances
- Clean inside microwave/crumb tray of toaster

Other

- Clean litter boxes/pet areas
- Mop/Sweep or vacuum the floors as needed

Weekly Cleaning Planner

Time	Monday

Time	Tuesday

Time	Wednesday

Time	Thursday

Time	Friday

Time	Saturday

Time	Sunday

Remarks / Goals

Daily Cleaning Checklist

Time   Week of: _____

Mon. Tue. Wed. Thu. Fri. Sat. Sun.

Bedrooms/Living Areas
- Make beds & Remove clutter - Straighten nightstand
- Put away clothing
- Vacuum or sweep as needed
- Straighten all pillows and blankets on the sofa
- Wipe spots and fingerprints from tabletops

Bathrooms
- Clean Mirror, the sink, faucet and other counter-top
- Squeegee or wipe shower door/curtain and walls
- Clean the toilet bowl & Wipe toilet seat / rim
- Replace any stained towels or washcloths

Kitchen
- Taking the trash out
- Wash dishes (load/Unload dishwasher)
- Wipe up spots on the floor & Sweep/mop as needed
- Clean sink, counter-tops, and appliances
- Clean inside microwave/crumb tray of toaster

Other
- Clean litter boxes/pet areas
- Mop/Sweep or vacuum the floors as needed

Weekly Cleaning Planner

Time	Monday		Time	Tuesday

Time	Wednesday		Time	Thursday

Time	Friday		Time	Saturday

Time	Sunday		Remarks / Goals	

Daily Cleaning Checklist

Time   Week of: _____

	Mon.	Tue.	Wed.	Thu.	Fri.	Sat.	Sun.

Bedrooms/Living Areas

- Make beds & Remove clutter - Straighten nightstand
- Put away clothing
- Vacuum or sweep as needed
- Straighten all pillows and blankets on the sofa
- Wipe spots and fingerprints from tabletops

Bathrooms

- Clean Mirror, the sink, faucet and other counter-top
- Squeegee or wipe shower door/curtain and walls
- Clean the toilet bowl & Wipe toilet seat / rim
- Replace any stained towels or washcloths

Kitchen

- Taking the trash out
- Wash dishes (load/Unload dishwasher)
- Wipe up spots on the floor & Sweep/mop as needed
- Clean sink, counter-tops, and appliances
- Clean inside microwave/crumb tray of toaster

Other

- Clean litter boxes/pet areas
- Mop/Sweep or vacuum the floors as needed

Weekly Cleaning Planner

Time	Monday		Time	Tuesday

Time	Wednesday		Time	Thursday

Time	Friday		Time	Saturday

Time	Sunday			Remarks / Goals

Daily Cleaning Checklist

Time   Week of: _____

	Mon.	Tue.	Wed.	Thu.	Fri.	Sat.	Sun.

Bedrooms/Living Areas
- Make beds & Remove clutter - Straighten nightstand
- Put away clothing
- Vacuum or sweep as needed
- Straighten all pillows and blankets on the sofa
- Wipe spots and fingerprints from tabletops

Bathrooms
- Clean Mirror, the sink, faucet and other counter-top
- Squeegee or wipe shower door/curtain and walls
- Clean the toilet bowl & Wipe toilet seat / rim
- Replace any stained towels or washcloths

Kitchen
- Taking the trash out
- Wash dishes (load/Unload dishwasher)
- Wipe up spots on the floor & Sweep/mop as needed
- Clean sink, counter-tops, and appliances
- Clean inside microwave/crumb tray of toaster

Other
- Clean litter boxes/pet areas
- Mop/Sweep or vacuum the floors as needed

Weekly Cleaning Planner

Time	Monday		Time	Tuesday

Time	Wednesday		Time	Thursday

Time	Friday		Time	Saturday

Time	Sunday		Remarks / Goals	

Daily Cleaning Checklist

Time   Week of:_____

	Mon.	Tue.	Wed.	Thu.	Fri.	Sat.	Sun.

Bedrooms/Living Areas

- Make beds & Remove clutter - Straighten nightstand
- Put away clothing
- Vacuum or sweep as needed
- Straighten all pillows and blankets on the sofa
- Wipe spots and fingerprints from tabletops

Bathrooms

- Clean Mirror, the sink, faucet and other counter-top
- Squeegee or wipe shower door/curtain and walls
- Clean the toilet bowl & Wipe toilet seat / rim
- Replace any stained towels or washcloths

Kitchen

- Taking the trash out
- Wash dishes (load/Unload dishwasher)
- Wipe up spots on the floor & Sweep/mop as needed
- Clean sink, counter-tops, and appliances
- Clean inside microwave/crumb tray of toaster

Other

- Clean litter boxes/pet areas
- Mop/Sweep or vacuum the floors as needed

Weekly Cleaning Planner

Time	Monday

Time	Tuesday

Time	Wednesday

Time	Thursday

Time	Friday

Time	Saturday

Time	Sunday

Remarks / Goals

Daily Cleaning Checklist

Time   Week of: _____   Mon. Tue. Wed. Thu. Fri. Sat. Sun.

Bedrooms/Living Areas

- Make beds & Remove clutter - Straighten nightstand
- Put away clothing
- Vacuum or sweep as needed
- Straighten all pillows and blankets on the sofa
- Wipe spots and fingerprints from tabletops

Bathrooms

- Clean Mirror, the sink, faucet and other counter-top
- Squeegee or wipe shower door/curtain and walls
- Clean the toilet bowl & Wipe toilet seat / rim
- Replace any stained towels or washcloths

Kitchen

- Taking the trash out
- Wash dishes (load/Unload dishwasher)
- Wipe up spots on the floor & Sweep/mop as needed
- Clean sink, counter-tops, and appliances
- Clean inside microwave/crumb tray of toaster

Other

- Clean litter boxes/pet areas
- Mop/Sweep or vacuum the floors as needed

Weekly Cleaning Planner

Time	Monday		Time	Tuesday

Time	Wednesday		Time	Thursday

Time	Friday		Time	Saturday

Time	Sunday		Remarks / Goals	

Daily Cleaning Checklist

Time   Week of: _____

	Mon.	Tue.	Wed.	Thu.	Fri.	Sat.	Sun.

Bedrooms/Living Areas
- Make beds & Remove clutter - Straighten nightstand
- Put away clothing
- Vacuum or sweep as needed
- Straighten all pillows and blankets on the sofa
- Wipe spots and fingerprints from tabletops

Bathrooms
- Clean Mirror, the sink, faucet and other counter-top
- Squeegee or wipe shower door/curtain and walls
- Clean the toilet bowl & Wipe toilet seat / rim
- Replace any stained towels or washcloths

Kitchen
- Taking the trash out
- Wash dishes (load/Unload dishwasher)
- Wipe up spots on the floor & Sweep/mop as needed
- Clean sink, counter-tops, and appliances
- Clean inside microwave/crumb tray of toaster

Other
- Clean litter boxes/pet areas
- Mop/Sweep or vacuum the floors as needed

Weekly Cleaning Planner

Time	Monday

Time	Tuesday

Time	Wednesday

Time	Thursday

Time	Friday

Time	Saturday

Time	Sunday

Remarks / Goals

Daily Cleaning Checklist

Time Week of: _____

	Mon.	Tue.	Wed.	Thu.	Fri.	Sat.	Sun.

Bedrooms/Living Areas

- Make beds & Remove clutter - Straighten nightstand
- Put away clothing
- Vacuum or sweep as needed
- Straighten all pillows and blankets on the sofa
- Wipe spots and fingerprints from tabletops

Bathrooms

- Clean Mirror, the sink, faucet and other counter-top
- Squeegee or wipe shower door/curtain and walls
- Clean the toilet bowl & Wipe toilet seat / rim
- Replace any stained towels or washcloths

Kitchen

- Taking the trash out
- Wash dishes (load/Unload dishwasher)
- Wipe up spots on the floor & Sweep/mop as needed
- Clean sink, counter-tops, and appliances
- Clean inside microwave/crumb tray of toaster

Other

- Clean litter boxes/pet areas
- Mop/Sweep or vacuum the floors as needed

Weekly Cleaning Planner

Time	Monday		Time	Tuesday

Time	Wednesday		Time	Thursday

Time	Friday		Time	Saturday

Time	Sunday		Remarks / Goals	

Daily Cleaning Checklist

Time   Week of: _____

	Mon.	Tue.	Wed.	Thu.	Fri.	Sat.	Sun.

Bedrooms/Living Areas

- Make beds & Remove clutter - Straighten nightstand
- Put away clothing
- Vacuum or sweep as needed
- Straighten all pillows and blankets on the sofa
- Wipe spots and fingerprints from tabletops

Bathrooms

- Clean Mirror, the sink, faucet and other counter-top
- Squeegee or wipe shower door/curtain and walls
- Clean the toilet bowl & Wipe toilet seat / rim
- Replace any stained towels or washcloths

Kitchen

- Taking the trash out
- Wash dishes (load/Unload dishwasher)
- Wipe up spots on the floor & Sweep/mop as needed
- Clean sink, counter-tops, and appliances
- Clean inside microwave/crumb tray of toaster

Other

- Clean litter boxes/pet areas
- Mop/Sweep or vacuum the floors as needed

Weekly Cleaning Planner

Time	Monday

Time	Tuesday

Time	Wednesday

Time	Thursday

Time	Friday

Time	Saturday

Time	Sunday

Remarks / Goals

Daily Cleaning Checklist

Time   Week of: _____

	Mon.	Tue.	Wed.	Thu.	Fri.	Sat.	Sun.

Bedrooms/Living Areas

- Make beds & Remove clutter - Straighten nightstand ☐☐☐☐☐☐☐
- Put away clothing ☐☐☐☐☐☐☐
- Vacuum or sweep as needed ☐☐☐☐☐☐☐
- Straighten all pillows and blankets on the sofa ☐☐☐☐☐☐☐
- Wipe spots and fingerprints from tabletops ☐☐☐☐☐☐☐

Bathrooms

- Clean Mirror, the sink, faucet and other counter-top ☐☐☐☐☐☐☐
- Squeegee or wipe shower door/curtain and walls ☐☐☐☐☐☐☐
- Clean the toilet bowl & Wipe toilet seat / rim ☐☐☐☐☐☐☐
- Replace any stained towels or washcloths ☐☐☐☐☐☐☐

Kitchen

- Taking the trash out ☐☐☐☐☐☐☐
- Wash dishes (load/Unload dishwasher) ☐☐☐☐☐☐☐
- Wipe up spots on the floor & Sweep/mop as needed ☐☐☐☐☐☐☐
- Clean sink, counter-tops, and appliances ☐☐☐☐☐☐☐
- Clean inside microwave/crumb tray of toaster ☐☐☐☐☐☐☐

Other

- Clean litter boxes/pet areas ☐☐☐☐☐☐☐
- Mop/Sweep or vacuum the floors as needed ☐☐☐☐☐☐☐

Weekly Cleaning Planner

Time	Monday		Time	Tuesday

Time	Wednesday		Time	Thursday

Time	Friday		Time	Saturday

Time	Sunday		Remarks / Goals	

Daily Cleaning Checklist

Time   Week of: _____

| | Mon. | Tue. | Wed. | Thu. | Fri. | Sat. | Sun. |

Bedrooms/Living Areas
- Make beds & Remove clutter - Straighten nightstand
- Put away clothing
- Vacuum or sweep as needed
- Straighten all pillows and blankets on the sofa
- Wipe spots and fingerprints from tabletops

Bathrooms
- Clean Mirror, the sink, faucet and other counter-top
- Squeegee or wipe shower door/curtain and walls
- Clean the toilet bowl & Wipe toilet seat / rim
- Replace any stained towels or washcloths

Kitchen
- Taking the trash out
- Wash dishes (load/Unload dishwasher)
- Wipe up spots on the floor & Sweep/mop as needed
- Clean sink, counter-tops, and appliances
- Clean inside microwave/crumb tray of toaster

Other
- Clean litter boxes/pet areas
- Mop/Sweep or vacuum the floors as needed

Weekly Cleaning Planner

Time	Monday		Time	Tuesday

Time	Wednesday		Time	Thursday

Time	Friday		Time	Saturday

Time	Sunday		Remarks / Goals	

Daily Cleaning Checklist

Time   Week of: _____

	Mon.	Tue.	Wed.	Thu.	Fri.	Sat.	Sun.

Bedrooms/Living Areas

- Make beds & Remove clutter - Straighten nightstand
- Put away clothing
- Vacuum or sweep as needed
- Straighten all pillows and blankets on the sofa
- Wipe spots and fingerprints from tabletops

Bathrooms

- Clean Mirror, the sink, faucet and other counter-top
- Squeegee or wipe shower door/curtain and walls
- Clean the toilet bowl & Wipe toilet seat / rim
- Replace any stained towels or washcloths

Kitchen

- Taking the trash out
- Wash dishes (load/Unload dishwasher)
- Wipe up spots on the floor & Sweep/mop as needed
- Clean sink, counter-tops, and appliances
- Clean inside microwave/crumb tray of toaster

Other

- Clean litter boxes/pet areas
- Mop/Sweep or vacuum the floors as needed

Weekly Cleaning Planner

Time	Monday		Time	Tuesday

Time	Wednesday		Time	Thursday

Time	Friday		Time	Saturday

Time	Sunday		Remarks / Goals	

Daily Cleaning Checklist

Time Week of: _____

	Mon.	Tue.	Wed.	Thu.	Fri.	Sat.	Sun.

Bedrooms/Living Areas
- Make beds & Remove clutter - Straighten nightstand
- Put away clothing
- Vacuum or sweep as needed
- Straighten all pillows and blankets on the sofa
- Wipe spots and fingerprints from tabletops

Bathrooms
- Clean Mirror, the sink, faucet and other counter-top
- Squeegee or wipe shower door/curtain and walls
- Clean the toilet bowl & Wipe toilet seat / rim
- Replace any stained towels or washcloths

Kitchen
- Taking the trash out
- Wash dishes (load/Unload dishwasher)
- Wipe up spots on the floor & Sweep/mop as needed
- Clean sink, counter-tops, and appliances
- Clean inside microwave/crumb tray of toaster

Other
- Clean litter boxes/pet areas
- Mop/Sweep or vacuum the floors as needed

Weekly Cleaning Planner

Time	Monday		Time	Tuesday

Time	Wednesday		Time	Thursday

Time	Friday		Time	Saturday

Time	Sunday		Remarks / Goals	

Daily Cleaning Checklist

Time   Week of: _____   Mon. Tue. Wed. Thu. Fri. Sat. Sun.

Bedrooms/Living Areas

- Make beds & Remove clutter - Straighten nightstand
- Put away clothing
- Vacuum or sweep as needed
- Straighten all pillows and blankets on the sofa
- Wipe spots and fingerprints from tabletops

Bathrooms

- Clean Mirror, the sink, faucet and other counter-top
- Squeegee or wipe shower door/curtain and walls
- Clean the toilet bowl & Wipe toilet seat / rim
- Replace any stained towels or washcloths

Kitchen

- Taking the trash out
- Wash dishes (load/Unload dishwasher)
- Wipe up spots on the floor & Sweep/mop as needed
- Clean sink, counter-tops, and appliances
- Clean inside microwave/crumb tray of toaster

Other

- Clean litter boxes/pet areas
- Mop/Sweep or vacuum the floors as needed

Weekly Cleaning Planner

Time	Monday		Time	Tuesday

Time	Wednesday		Time	Thursday

Time	Friday		Time	Saturday

Time	Sunday		Remarks / Goals	

Daily Cleaning Checklist

Time   Week of: _____

| | Mon. | Tue. | Wed. | Thu. | Fri. | Sat. | Sun. |

Bedrooms/Living Areas

- Make beds & Remove clutter – Straighten nightstand
- Put away clothing
- Vacuum or sweep as needed
- Straighten all pillows and blankets on the sofa
- Wipe spots and fingerprints from tabletops

Bathrooms

- Clean Mirror, the sink, faucet and other counter-top
- Squeegee or wipe shower door/curtain and walls
- Clean the toilet bowl & Wipe toilet seat / rim
- Replace any stained towels or washcloths

Kitchen

- Taking the trash out
- Wash dishes (load/Unload dishwasher)
- Wipe up spots on the floor & Sweep/mop as needed
- Clean sink, counter-tops, and appliances
- Clean inside microwave/crumb tray of toaster

Other

- Clean litter boxes/pet areas
- Mop/Sweep or vacuum the floors as needed

Weekly Cleaning Planner

Time	Monday		Time	Tuesday

Time	Wednesday		Time	Thursday

Time	Friday		Time	Saturday

Time	Sunday		Remarks / Goals	

Daily Cleaning Checklist

Time   Week of: _____   Mon. Tue. Wed. Thu. Fri. Sat. Sun.

Bedrooms/Living Areas

- Make beds & Remove clutter - Straighten nightstand
- Put away clothing
- Vacuum or sweep as needed
- Straighten all pillows and blankets on the sofa
- Wipe spots and fingerprints from tabletops

Bathrooms

- Clean Mirror, the sink, faucet and other counter-top
- Squeegee or wipe shower door/curtain and walls
- Clean the toilet bowl & Wipe toilet seat / rim
- Replace any stained towels or washcloths

Kitchen

- Taking the trash out
- Wash dishes (load/Unload dishwasher)
- Wipe up spots on the floor & Sweep/mop as needed
- Clean sink, counter-tops, and appliances
- Clean inside microwave/crumb tray of toaster

Other

- Clean litter boxes/pet areas
- Mop/Sweep or vacuum the floors as needed

Weekly Cleaning Planner

Time	Monday

Time	Tuesday

Time	Wednesday

Time	Thursday

Time	Friday

Time	Saturday

Time	Sunday

Remarks / Goals

Monthly Cleaning Checklist

- Dust all blinds
- Vacuum under furniture/ sofa cushions
- Dust baseboards
- Dust ceiling fans, air vents and light fixtures
- Wash out trashcans
- Vacuum basement
- Organize all closets
- Clean window treatments
- Check smoke alarms & change filters
- Deep clean appliances
- Wash blankets
- Wipe down fridge shelves
- Bathing pets

Monthly Cleaning Checklist

Seasonal Cleaning Checklist

- Changing the air filters.
- Changing Batteries on detectors. (carbon monoxide/smoke)
- Clean/Disinfect keyboards, mouse and remote controls.
- Dust all Sealing tile grout or stone and concrete counter-tops
- Clean outside accessory items such as patio furniture
- Clean Fire place
- Move fridge, vacuum and mop behind it, vacuum coils on fridge
- Flip/rotate Mattress.
- Check expiration date on fire extinguisher
- Disposing properly of old medicines. Reviewing emergency kits
- Wash and/or replace shower liners and shower curtains. Dust the rods
- Trim shrubbery, prune trees.
- Put away out-of-season clothes, pull out seasonally appropriate clothing.
- Wipe walls, touch up paint & vacuum books.
- Discard old and expired makeup. Clean your makeup holders
- Deep clean your fridge and freezer. If needed, defrost freezer.
- Shred sensitive documents you don't need anymore.
- Polish silver jewelry, silverware, and any other tarnished items.
- Organize shoes
- Dust china in china cabinet
- Shampoo rugs or carpet
- Clean dryer vent, clean washing machine, and clean lint trap
- Donate unneeded clothing and toys
- Clean & sanitize plastic toys, wash stuffed animals and soft toys
- Clean & organize the garage
- Purge anything stored under bed you don't want anymore.
- Clean and disinfect tub and shower
- Remove cobwebs
- Dust light fixtures and ceiling fans
- Clean window tracks and screens
- Sweep and mop under washer and dryer
- Check and repair sprinklers
- Inspect roof tiles / shingles

Seasonal Cleaning Checklist

Scrub porch ceiling, floors and walls

Update home inventory, review insurance policies

Special Care Cleaning Instructions

Item/Surface

Material   Notes
Cleaner
Tools
Stains
Store

Item/Surface

Material   Notes
Cleaner
Tools
Stains
Store

Item/Surface

Material   Notes
Cleaner
Tools
Stains
Store

Item/Surface

Material   Notes
Cleaner
Tools
Stains
Store

Item/Surface

Material   Notes
Cleaner
Tools
Stains
Store

Special Care Cleaning Instructions

Item/Surface

Material	Notes
Cleaner	
Tools	
Stains	
Store	

Item/Surface

Material	Notes
Cleaner	
Tools	
Stains	
Store	

Item/Surface

Material	Notes
Cleaner	
Tools	
Stains	
Store	

Item/Surface

Material	Notes
Cleaner	
Tools	
Stains	
Store	

Item/Surface

Material	Notes
Cleaner	
Tools	
Stains	
Store	

Homemade Cleaners Formulas

Ingredients	Instructions

Ingredients	Instructions

Ingredients	Instructions

Ingredients	Instructions

Laundry Schedule

Monday	
Tuesday	
Wednesday	
Thursday	
Friday	
Saturday	
Sunday	

All rights reserved. No part of this publication may be reproduced, distributed, or transmitted in any form or by any means, including photocopying, recording, or other electronic or mechanical methods, without the prior written permission of the publisher, except in the case of brief quotations embodied in critical reviews and certain other noncommercial uses permitted by copyright law.

Designed & created with the help of resources from: freepik.com, freepik.com/olga-spb.

Made in the USA
Coppell, TX
08 January 2024

27409709R00070